A SOUL RESTORATION PLAN TO TAKE YOUR LIFE FROM

Distress to Success

An Instrument of Divine Intervention
"He Restoreth My Soul"

Paula A. Price, PhD

Unless otherwise indicated, all scriptural quotations are from the King James Version of the Bible.

3D Distress to Success Healing and Deliverance Process Plan

Flaming Vision Publications

Tulsa, Oklahoma 74136

ISBN 1-886288-14-3

Printed in the United States of America

A SOUL RESTORATION PLAN TO TAKE YOUR LIFE FROM

Your Spiritual Freedom Guide

Your Name:

Program Start Date:

Program End Date:

TABLE OF TOPICS

THE PROCESS

Take Your Life From:

Ⓑ Stands for 3 Dimensional: **Decision, Discovery, Deliverance**

Congratulations on your decision to restore your life. Your being here covers the first 'D" of the 3D's. That is, decision. You made the decision to stop committing slow suicide and restore your life and world to wholeness. The second 'D' is discovery, the next stage. That is where you sift your soul and your actions to discover how you got to this place in your life. It will be the hardest part because it forces you to face some very unpleasant things about how you think, feel, believe and behave. These are all the strongholds that reinforce your addiction. Discovery, by the way, is the longest phase of the process. How you respond to the discovery phase of your process determines when real healing ultimately begins. This process involves mining your soul for insights that present you with the keys to living free and healthy. Diligent *soul mining* is the only way to obtain the answers that repossess your freewill. The last 'D' is the reward, deliverance. Should you tackle and conquer the discovery phase of the process, you will be rewarded with deliverance, explained at length in other sections of your guide.

Decision: Restoring your life and world to wholeness.

At this point, just know that you are now engaged in a one of a kind process to retake the power over your life. You are going to walk through a series of stages and phases that culminate in you stepping out of addiction into Divine Purpose. Everything you do during this time hinges on your taking responsibility for your present. It is the only way to void your past covenants with death and destruction. This is a must for you to acquire and act on the principles that secure your new life and liberty in the Lord Jesus Christ. Otherwise, you will never permanently regain control of your future, no matter how many times you try.

If you fail to meet the Lord's deliverance and healing demands, the closing years of your life may well be filled with the start and stop merry go round you have been on so far. Ending the cycle is the only way to reclaim your soul and recover your personhood. When you have completed your initial healing and deliverance process, you need to set up regular contacts with a PPM Global Resources Adviser to train you to live free. The information on this step will be provided for you at the end of this stage of your journey.

I wish you the best and pray the Lord's strength, courage, conviction and wisdom bring you to victory. God bless you; now, let's get to work.

Sincerely,

Dr. Paula A. Price, PhD
And Your ❸ Soul Restoration Team

To enjoy outward success, you must have *inward* success.
Your soul is your life's success center.
Dr. Paula Price

THE SOUL RESTORATION PLAN OUTLINE

My Success Coach:

Office:	**Phone**:

Office Hours:	**Email**

Overview
3D Orientation

This is a Soul Restoration Plan that guides you through the process of taking your life from Distress to Success. As you move through it, these words will come to mean a great deal to you. Taking you to the root of your addiction, which iswas relinquishing your freewill to serve your body's destruction, sets you on the path of deliverance. The 3D Plan teaches you how to repossess your freewill in order to lead a healthy and productive life. The means by which this is accomplished is by training you to transform your soul's death codes to the codes of life. In doing so, you get to command it to issue and sustain your emotional well being.

Every session puts you in touch with your soul's liberating truths, because truth alone holds the power to set a captive free. Truth has many layers, almost as many layers as your skin. There is eternal truth, moral truth, mortal truth, heavenly truth, and earthly truth. To be free from your addicton, you must consider your emotional truth, integrity and honesty: How real is your desire to be free? And how badly do you want it? Social and cultural truth all contributed to your addiction, and then there is your personal truth. What is this you ask? It is the truth that took you captive and convinced you to choose addiction to treat your soul issues. Frankly speaking, it is that truth and only that truth that will set you free indeed; enter the 3D Soul Restoration Plan. Many soul captives do not know that not any truth persuaded them to surrender to the spiritual stronghold of their addiction and not just any truth can set them free from it. Your journey through the 3D process will guide your soul mining so that you will recall the lie that enslaved you because it must be recalled to set you free from your addiction. Every convincing truth that sold you on your enslavement must be examined, even if they are not all equal in scope and effect. But what is personal truth?

Personal truth is your soul's rationale for your captivity. The reason it backfired is because your circumstantial or relative truth, as some call it, clashed with God's creature truths. This happens because what enslaves a soul is its version of what damaged it. The soul's tale baited the addiction and can now be known as its personal truth insofar as its dependency or compulsion goes.

The 3D Plan teaches you how to repossess your freewill in order to lead a healthy and productive life.

The goal of the 3D Process is to uncover the truth that will make *you* free. That may be different from the truth that sets another soul free. Many earthly truths are relative, but are not equal to heavenly truths. Eternal and heavenly truths carry infinitely greater weight and so must inevitably be obeyed to avoid or reverse their consequences. Ignoring these heavenly truths is what enslaved your soul. Your conflict with them formed the basis for the personal truth that led you to believer you could snub them without repercussions.

Personal truth is relative to your life, your world, your wounds, and your healing. In the same way that not all medicines heal everybody, so it is with truth. What hurt you and sent you on your destructive course of life may not have even phased someone else.

That is why you must give diligent attention to the second 'D' in the 3D Process: discovery.

To liberate your soul, you must break the seal on your own stronghold to uncover not only what happened to you, but why it affected you so drastically or destructively. That answer is key to separating your heart and soul from your addiction. This statement is made with exception being given to those soul traumas that make people victims of horrible life events. Innocent victims of inhuman atrocities have soul strongholds that respond to truth's deliverance in other ways. These will be addressed throughout the process. Whatever the gateway, the 3D Process aims to achieve its ultimate outcome, which is to:

"Give your soul the power to free itself to succeed."

THE PREMISE

The **D** Distress to Success Soul Restoration Plan is systemic and systematic. It uses a walk it out, work it out approach that differs from many other comparable programs. Most of them concentrate largely on talking it out. The 3D Plan rests on the overriding principle that people make intelligent decisions to addict their souls, even if the processes that seduced them to do so are hidden from them. Scripture says that as a person thinks in the heart so is he or she. What it means in respect to your soul's captivity and

deliverance is that it all began in your heart. It is in their heart's that people think themselves into addicting and from there talk themselves into it. In moments of despair, they imagine long standing ways to ease their emotional pain that restrain its memory. In the process they evaluate numerous options to find the one that fits their case. Once that is decided on, whether it is ice cream and sweets, alcohol, deceits or abuse, etc., they select it and move on to the next step in their soul's remedy. The common thread that ties it all together is knowledge: They risk addiction because they want to know why they hurt. They want to know how to stop the hurting. They want to know how to ease their burdens in life. They want to know how to push forward with minimum pain and suffering. And, they want to know how to feel good more often and longer than they feel bad.

Intelligent logic, however distorted it may be, lays at the heart of all addictions which, by the way, starts in the heart. Solutional rationales went into the addict's decision to find answers to questions that keep them in the game of life as pain free as possible.

> **To put it bluntly, people talk themselves into becoming addicted for the sake of expedience; it serves their emotional, professional, relational, or medicinal expedience.**

To get free from a soul bondage, they must have a more intelligent reason to talk themselves out of it. Becoming a soul abuser made sense to the addict on some level. Therefore, liberating the soul from authorized dependencies must make more sense than the rationale used to justify the addiction, and the 3D Plan does just that. This Soul Restoration Plan aims to overturn enslavement by laying the ax to the root of your dependency in order to end your spiritual captivity. When one refers to laying the ax to the root, biblically speaking, one is talking about systemically addressing the source as well as the cause of an issue.

RESTORING THE SOUL

Focusing on the soul's condition and assaults is the only way to restore a life because the soul's function is complex and affects the entire human makeup. A contaminated soul can only contaminate its life. A soul whose root system is tainted will also only yield tainted fruit in life. How the addict viewed himself or herself when life hit hard, long ago laid down life choice tracks that legitimized the compulsion. Going through your 3D Guide progressively makes these realities clear to you because by now they have gotten lost in your addiction.

Think On This:
Liberating yourself must make more sense than the rationale used to keep you bound.

ABOUT YOUR GUIDE

The 3D Distress to Success Guide is thoroughly explained under its own heading where its purpose, value and the other materials listed in it are described.

The 3D Process Description

A series of sessions devoted to Living Addiction Free based on the process outlined in the Healing and Deliverance Guide.

3D Goals

- 3D Introduce the 3D Process and how participants will be engaged in it.
- 3D Review the objectives as stated in the goals.
- 3D Proceed to work with participant using the Distress to Success Guide

3D users come declaring "Enough is enough."

Requirements:

See the *'Materials'* section of your Healing and Deliverance Guide.

Resources:

See the *'Process Supplements'* in your Healing and Deliverance Guide.

Evaluating Soul Restoration Success:

- 3D Conformance to process healing and deliverance requirements
- 3D Completion of all assigned Guide Transformation Tasks
- 3D Evidence of process objectives in action

BEST 3D PROCESS USERS

Every betterment program has a best user group: the type of people that benefit more readily from it than others. Best users bind to the program quickly, rapidly assimilate its content, and responsively apply its wisdoms to their lives. In short, they learn and act on its instructions faster than most. These 3D participants profit almost immediately from what they receive. When it comes to best users, The 3D Soul Restoration Plan is no different.

While it is adaptable and efficacious with many types of addicts or captives, it is more immediately effective with those whose attitudes about their addiction is settled. These people enter the sessions with one thing on their minds: "Enough is enough." The person fed up with the bondage, the up and down, and on again off again roller coaster of detoxification and retoxification is the perfect candidate for the 3D Process. Should that person happen to be a Christian, all the better.

So what does this mean? It means that 3D is useful to anyone struggling with addiction, but it can be most uniquely and enduringly effective with those who have resolved in their

Enough Is Enough

heart to become free. 3D's principles and discoveries speedily penetrate its participants' souls to enlighten them on how to remain free and how to make their deliverance permanent. Subsequent encounters with the 3D Process go on to instruct succeeders on how to live addiction free. Once they have made up their minds to beat their addiction, those who enroll in 3D with these resolves firmly embedded in their souls will do whatever it takes to reach their goal. When a person turns to something like the 3D Plan for help, it is to learn how to *enforce* their rejection of the addiction on the spiritual power reinforcing it. Instinctively, the most compatible 3D candidates realize that it takes more than words, wishing, or hoping to be free. They know it takes deep soul work and great discomfort to succeed. And, they are braced for it. The 'enough is enough' group looks forward to facing and defeating their soul's captor for the very last time, and their incoming communications show it.

> *"The 'enough is enough' group knows it takes deep soul work and great discomfort to succeed and are braced for it."*

The 3D Plan's biblical foundation makes it more suitable to the Christian struggling with residual addictions, lingering compulsions or traumas. Later discussions explain this further. Thus, it is useful to the pastor over the local church, the minister over a ministry network, marketplace ministers to help their workers recover from dependency and soul wounds, and any other Christian entity looking to invoke the healing and deliverance power of the Lord Jesus Christ.

The 3D Process can easily be used in the church by all ministers, but it is especially suited to counselors, healers, and deliverance ministers. The Plan's orderly presentment of the principles and procedures for setting the captive soul free provides spiritual liberators with an organized means of releasing a person from their soul bondage. The process blends Scripture, The Holy Spirit, God's Logos and Rhema, Prayer and Prophecy, and Human Insight with practical (and doable) soul wisdom. It engages the intellect and the sentiments to succeed.

DISCLAIMER

The 3D Soul Restoration Plan to Take Your Soul from Distress to Success is a spiritual and not a clinical approach. It uses God's healing and deliverance to root out systemic addiction and other soul entanglements. It dispenses a wholly biblical approach to delivering you from your addiction. The Plan is based on scripture's knowledge of the spiritual moorings of a soul's bondage.

For these reasons, the 3D Restoration Plan does not seek to take the place of clinical detoxification treatment because it is expressly designed to follow it. Proven clinical therapies should not be rejected and replaced with 3D. Clients who are certain that the medical and organic roots of their addiction have been resolved need to obtain written confirmation of this from an authorized practitioner. The 3D Process is particularly designed to be a supplement or a final step in the process of taking an enslaved life from Distress to Success.

Stage 1

SOUL RESTORATION DISTRESS TO SUCCESS FOUNDATION

What's Covered:

- If I be lifted up
- The Christ Distinctive
- The New Creation Spirit
- The Path to Dependency
- The Addict's Intelligence
- How God Delivers a Soul
- 3D Integrity and Fidelity
- 3D Is for You

UNDERSTANDING THE 3D PROCESS

Jesus said, "If I be lifted up I will draw all men unto me." The Christian church has narrowed that all-pervasive statement down to mainly evangelism. Its position on it is to get the lost saved and churched, and then turn them over to everything outside of it to rid them of their suffering. While it is popular to tout a Christian worldview or a Christian perspective, to some ministers those are mere words. Many of them have limited it to His power to save and inwardly question His power to heal and deliver. After all, they ask, how much can Jesus' really antiquated message apply to modern soul bondage?

Numerous ministry programs, ostensibly enlisted to heal suffering souls, merely slap Christ's name on them and promote them as church run programs. Precious few of them bother to weave little more than His name throughout the material they use to treat a soul's maladies. Christ's doctrines, perspectives, and insights are frequently omitted in order to not offend the unbelieving and attract a larger following. The 3D Plan decided on an approach that promises Christ's fullest benefits. It did so knowing that, overtly or covertly, He is the world's only true soul liberator. Still, they need more than His words. Soul captives need His wisdom, His will, and His powerful Holy Spirit to get set free. The 3D Process delivers on all three.

THE CHRIST DISTINCTIVE

In far too many cases, much of what is done to heal believers from addiction closely resembles what all sick souls get outside of

Christ. When it comes to the genuine Christian, these methods fall woefully short of the Lord Jesus' "free indeed" credo. Addicts' destructive habits are temporarily modified, but the stronghold sustaining the addiction remains unaffected. Here is why-salvation deposits Christ within His converts. It literally installs Him behind their souls. Besides that, salvation's redemption brings with it a heavenly quality of life that leaves His converts only scarcely affected by humanist treatments. Jesus' Holy Spirit within causes new creation spirits to resist carnal remedies. That effect is what being born of God means.

Through the Risen Lord Jesus Christ, the Almighty constantly acts on the souls He indwells. The imperceptible new birth, that is far too often treated insignificantly, shows itself most when old ways are imposed on it. Then it reacts to fend off threats to its divine attributes and virtues, and so neutralizes humanist efforts in the end. When the new creation soul comes under assault, the superlativeness of being a new creature in Christ Jesus is aroused. It so aggressively resists being muted or frustrated, that human measures used to treat it lose their effectiveness over time. The enslaved Christian gets caught in an agonizing cycle of temporary relief and recidivism as a result.

MORE THAN EXORCISM

Another major but misleading church view on addiction is that all a bound soul needs is an exorcism to be delivered. Cast out the devil and the lifelong abuser, addict, or oppressed saint will be immediately and eternally set free. Rarely does it happen that way. That is not to say that it never happens because I am one of those for whom it did. It is to say that most people need more than a one step treatment plan to remain addiction free. They need to be taught how to "think free" in order to live free, and both take time.

Total healing and deliverance also takes intelligence because what caught the soul in its addictive web engaged the heart's intelligence. This is what Paul means by 2 Corinthians 10:1-6. The reason exorcism is frequently not enough is because addiction emerges from a highly sentient and often intelligent soul. Addiction appeals to those striving to address unbearable heart issues that most people in the addict's life do not see or just ignore. Oftentimes, an "I'll fix it myself" or "I'll show them" sentiment sets the dependency solution in motion and schedules it for future addiction. The moment those thoughts settle in the heart, every emotion felt or appetite craved gathers the momentum to become the ultimate answer to a long standing unbearable pain or passion. The damaged soul that was ignored begins to stop its pain with drastic measures that only lead to the demolition of its world.

A BROKEN HEART DAMAGES THE SOUL

People's emotional suffering starts in their heart from which, the Lord says, come the "issues of life". If they are not reconnected with the heartache that damaged their soul, people will remain addicted because it is a defense mechanism they devised to make it through life and to make life make more sense. Remember this as the addicts or compulsives murky logic. In the end the goal of the self medication or obsessive conduct is to make sense out a painful life ordeal that will not stop hurting. The objective of the soul's emotional agonies is to devise pain relievers that numb the feelings and shove down the torment.

The last, but the most resolute, instrument in people's decision to addict is their human will. Willpower initiated the contract they made with the temptation that brought them into bondage. Soul demolishing spirits control addicts by permission. Until they withdraw that permission, efforts to liberate them are futile. The reason is, because unknown to many, addiction is a legal contract. For all of these reasons, the 3D Soul Restoration Plan actively engages its participants whole being in the deliverance process. It uses relevant education and wisdom to raise participants' human will to become and remain addiction free. Education is the gateway to everything in society: why should it be dismissed when people are trying to reenter the world of an addiction free life.

THE PATH TO DEPENDENCY

No matter how deep beneath the subconscious it is made, the decision to treat a soul's sorrow addictively comes from a smart mind. It is deliberate and calculating. Great thought goes into easing any pain, especially a soul's pain. Not just any solution will do. Soul relief addictions can appear long after what caused its pain happened. That is why there is an intellectual disconnect when their negative effects show up to replace earlier failed attempts to erase a trauma. Before dependency set in, numerous little tactics blacked out hurtful memories, blocked emotional pain, and guaranteed pleasure in their place. Virtually harmless at first, the replacements steadily increased the demand for stronger and stronger, longer lasting measures. The outcome was your dependency on what made you hurt less and feel good the longest. Both outcomes, brought about through constant self medicating, paved the road to your full blown addiction way back when dependency was the farthest thing from your mind.

DISAPPOINTMENT - THE BIG 'D' IN ADDICTION

There are many reasons for addictions and compulsions. A deeper look at them will surface a single common denominator: disappointment. The word *disappointment* includes

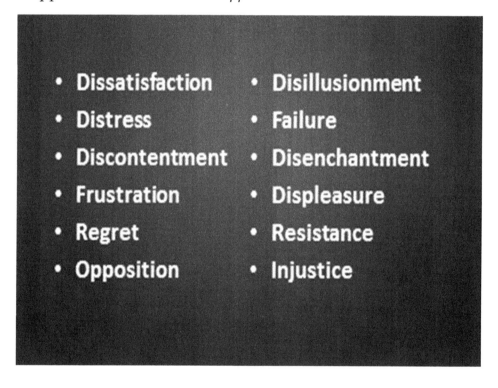

These are all caused by:

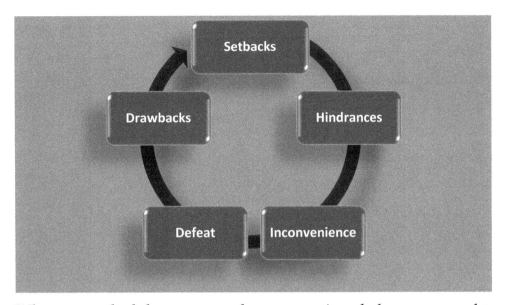

Whatever ordeal that overtaxed your emotions led to your need to retreat to survive or suppress it. You can be assured that disappointment is at the root of it. The nature and circumstances of that disappointment must be discovered and dismantled to free your soul. Here are some helpful starter questions: Who or what broke your heart? Who or what stifled your hope? Who or what lifted you up, abruptly let you down, and left you with no recourse? These questions should be explored to begin the process of getting to the root of your addiction's logic. It is the only way to map out its pathway. Its mysteries must be traced from heart to soul, soul to will, will to mind, and mind to body if you are going to break free from it.

Considering that addiction is a consolation or flight response to soul sorrow, it manifests blatant or subtle reactions to frustration. Not to negate the organic causes that are discussed elsewhere, the bedrock of all emotional disturbances is locked in some kind of disappointment. To bury its magnitude within the soul for any number of reasons, some people choose to paint another picture of the hurtful event for the outside world that masks it. The cover story used to lessen the blow is constructed in a way that lets a disturbed soul live with a staggering letdown or its consequences. At the same time, the coverup frees the otherwise taunting thoughts and recollections to sidestep them and press on with life. Look at some examples of very familiar, yet quite impactful, disappointing blows that can destabilize a life:

- Disappointment with family or friends
- Constantly broken promises or missed opportunities
- Regret of poor life choices that cost more than expected
- Repeated failures and perceived injustice
- Loss of a loved one or a vital companion
- Broken dreams and delayed life plans
- Inequity, under privileged, or downtrodden
- Abuse by authority figures
- Impossible obstacles due to family limitations
- Unbeatable odds from being confined to a poor neighborhood
- Poverty and setbacks
- Shattered relationships
- Abandonment, neglect, rejection
- Senseless alienation, loneliness

Of the fourteen examples, the last five reinforce disappointment. Abandonment, neglect, rejection, alienation, and loneliness. All of these stem from a failed expectation. *Abandonment*, the abrupt departure of someone loved or relied on, or the failure of one entrusted to fulfill a duty or responsibility. *Neglect*, an expectation of care and attention that was denied or diverted to others. *Rejection*, anticipating being accepted, but being spurned and refused instead. The disappointment root holds true even in the case of crime, abuse, or violent assaults.

To explain further, the crime victim must get over being alone and defenseless and violently exploited because of it. That soul must cease, or at least curtail, reliving a helpless cry that went unheard and a horrific assault where no one came to its rescue. Something else must take suffering's place and console the painful recollection. As you can see, several things can burden the weakened soul. Here are some for you to consider.

1. Lack of people to care
2. Lack of emotional pain relief
3. Lack of needed protection
4. Lack of defense
5. Lack of provision
6. Lack of rescue

Every one of these, and no doubt more besides them, fuels the disappointment that fuses with abandonment, neglect, and aloneness. When left to run their couse, they manacle the soul to rejection and bind it to alienation and dispair. Here are a few more for you to consider.

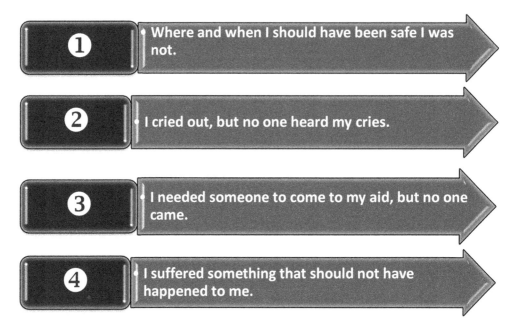

In the above scenarios, the physical abuse was bad enough, but the mistrust it breeds brings the ongoing torment. The next page voices a few more of the soul's frustrations that keep it locked in a cycle of torment.

Thought Notes

_____

_____

_____

_____

_____

_____

_____

Humans should not treat each other that way.

 Why me; what did I do to deserve evil when I expected good.

 How is it that I failed to see this or that in the person I married, dated, worked with and so on?

 How could I have been so stupid?

 I ruined my life; now what can I do about it?

A Few Thoughts I Have on this Insight:

Share your thoughts on this discussion.

_____

_____

_____

_____

_____

_____

HEAD NOISE

Head noise is the constant drone of memories or other torments going off in your head. They are constant because whenever silence comes you realize they never shut up. These pounding thoughts amount to self disappointment. They swirl around in your head when you expect something to turn out well, but all your anticipations go unfulfilled. Haunted by the ordeal and bothered by the inability to put it behind them, the strongholds end up imprisoning some people to constant disappointment. The reason is they feel they should be back in the stream of life but find themselves barely able to believe for anything anymore. Senseless alienation and loneliness are the end products of the previous three. They are the results of waiting expectantly until time and disappointment convince you to abandon your hope.

Where was God? Why did He let this or that happen to me?

The granddaddy of the disappointment stream is, of course, God. Where was He? Why did He let this or that happen to me? Why did He not stop it? What did I do to make Him not step in for me?

Issues that bring about these reactions are hardest on Christians because the totality of their lives, past, present and future is bound up in their hope in God. Their faith teachings groom them to expect Him to save them from all of life's ups and downs, all the time, no matter what. They believe it is His primary duty to prevent their world from shattering. When He does not, spiritual and emotional disappointment sets in that can lead them to feel rejected by Him for reasons they cannot fathom or do little about in the end.

In retaliation for His perceived abandonment, these Christians fall into addiction or some other compulsion because they decide to replace the Lord with other consolations and protection. A little bit of revenge and a whole lot of dejection makes them do so. This is when the idolatry option comes to the table, although many would be loathe to admit it. These souls disguise their decision to evict God from their lives as something innocent. When in effect they just opted to change their god.

Busyness, work, family, hobbies, career, or in the extreme, another god, or worse, atheism took the Lord's place to punish Him for not being there when the sufferer needed Him. Others make the same decision naively unaware of their resolve to live their life their own way on their own terms. They choose to exist without Christ in their lives, or they adopt another deity in His place. Either way, deliberately making themselves unaccountable to the Lord inevitably yields futile, and sometimes fatal, results. When the Savior is dismissed, it creates a spiritual gap that has to be filled with something, and that something is your addiction or compulsion. You will explore this subtlety later under the heading of Addiction Academics.

SOURCING OUT THE DISAPPOINTING ISSUE

Getting to the root of any one or combination of the issues we've discussed may seem easy. After all, they have already been identified as disappointment, haven't they? But that is not all that

33

it takes. Humans are complex creatures. Ambivalence and ambiguity mark most of their life choices and actions. Look at some of their most perplexing contradictions:

D₃

- Humans are intelligent and unenlightened at the same time.
- They know what they feel, but cannot say *why* they feel it.
- They know what hurts them, but cannot understand why it does.

- They know what they want out of life, but are at a loss as to how to get it without disappointment.
- They know they have a purpose that should fulfill their destiny, but cannot plot the right path to it.

What plagues the average person can be obvious and vague at once, and both appear logical and irrational. What can benefit so many people in life can also devastate them, which makes a snap one step deliverance out of the question. People's bondage may be a devil, but he is not the only creature in their life's drama or the lone source of their addiction. For instance, a spirit may know the soul buttons to push or the heart strings to pluck, but it is the person's will that must make and keep the right button or string available. An intricate cast of characters holds people together and attends to their captivity. These mysterious figures must be thoughtfully disclosed (and dislodged) in order to set a captive soul free. Doing so calls for a great deal of the suffering soul's involvement. As you read on, you will comprehend why this is the case and accept that in most situations it will take more than a prayer and a command to make you free.

MORE THAN A PRAYER

As far as the larger faith population goes, deliverance typically takes more than a highly charged church service where prolonged wrestling with devils takes place. Arduous efforts go into expelling devils, and that calls for more than prayerful incantations. While that is a good start, in the end, it takes wisdom to liberate a captive soul completely because people are intelligent and many addicts are highly intelligent. Just look at the genius they engage to trick their communities and families into supporting their addictions. Cunning excuses, accusations, and deflections are invented to enforce their decision to opt out of life.

Shrewdly, addicts and compulsives sell their world on their need to escape into a mental fairyland. Believable arguments and tactics free them from the burdens of life most people refuse to avoid. Addicts skillfully sell others on the depth of their sorrow and their incompatibility with life in general. They claim their reluctant retreat into addiction is the ultimate response to a world that just does not get them. They are persuaded that dependency is all they have left after a long list of ineffective ways that failed to bring them out of the pain and sorrow afflicting their souls. The addiction is portrayed as a last ditch effort to feel good, and its fallout, not of their doing. Amazingly, they convince people, sometimes for years, that they are not addicts, but merely working through difficult times. The dependency gets them through, and, in no time at all, they will be fine. All they need is time to get it together. With slick words and a pretended sincerity, they enlist their loved ones help and support to finance them bowing out on life. The ploy works not only because the addict is a clever deceiver, but also because those closest to them would rather not believe a loved one or trusted friend is indeed addicted, let alone misusing them.

THE ADDICT'S INTELLIGENCE

The intelligence to get a single person to finance a lifestyle of addiction takes a remarkable salesperson. To get one's entire family to tolerate it, to its own peril, is commendable. However, to get a circle of friends and supporters to join that group is incredible. And how about this? To hide an addiction for months or years while displaying its signs so blatantly that those close to you should have detected them is stupendous. Add to these, the masterful deceits that keep the trusting entangled in a web of lies, if for no other reason than their love for the addict is stupefying. Again, it works because loving family and friends do not want to believe their beloved is caught in such a destructive trap. That disbelief indulges all of the mayhem caused by the addict, and prolongs the decision to be set free from it.

All of this is to say that the discernment and Creator related principles required to deliver a soul from any bondage begin with the Maker and not with the thing made, which is why 3D works best with those filled with Christ's Spirit. It is also why Christian resources and elements are used to pierce the soul and expose the captive force facilitating the addiction.

Heart ⮂Soul ⮂ Mind ⮂ Impact: Ⅾ₃

Share your thoughts on this discussion.

_____

_____

_____

_____

_____

_____

_____

_____

_____

_____

_____

HOW GOD DELIVERS A SOUL

God's Spirit employs earthly tools one way for the unsaved and another way for the saved. His residence within the redeemed responds to the codes of life the new birth installs in a particular manner. Being outside of a suffering human requires the Holy Spirit to address their issues from an entirely different vantage point, with every action deliberately implemented to lead the person to salvation. It is true that both groups must begin with repentance; however, it is the type and the effect of the repentance that separates them. The unsaved must repent to receive the forgiveness that slaughters the old man and implants the new creature in Christ Jesus in its place. The addicted saved must repent of idolatry and the waywardness that preceded it. The unsaved addict must enter God's family; the addicted saved must deal with mistreating Him as a member of it. None of these statements aim to discredit non-Christian programs; they are only to validate the spiritual premises of the 3D Process. Read on to see how this happens.

> *"God's Spirit employs earthly tools one way for the unsaved and another way for the saved."*

Another reason that 3D declares its Christian anchor so boldly has to do with how the world conditioned its citizens to disdain Christ and Christianity. A massive campaign has worked overtime to discredit both. People learn in school, from the media, and in their games how to hate anything Christian. Without realizing it, many of them recoil from even the idea of having their addictions treated by Jesus Christ, and it is not only unbelievers who do this. The mere mention of the name of Jesus in this era unleashes a programmed contempt that moves reflexively to shut the soul sufferer down. Many addicts are so brainwashed by the campaign against Him that they do not realize that the principles used by other like programs began with Him. Consequently, much of what sets a captive soul free today is founded upon His doctrines, teachings, and principles; they just take His name out of it.

ANOTHER THOUGHT

You need to recognize that if you have been chemically dependent for ages, you have run your body down. You no doubt have allergies, nutritional deficits, and distorted appetites that came from depriving yourself of healthy meals. Poor eating apart from addiction is detrimental to your body; how much more damaging is replacing meals with toxic chemicals. Therefore, another solution you should add to your addiction free therapies is a holistic health regimen. You should connect with a health and nutrition expert to add their advice and treatments to your 3D Plan. This is important for another reason. It may be that poor childhood eating habits or your mother's unhealthy appetites contributed to your addiction proclivities. Had they been discovered earlier in your life, you may have been spared your present distress. This is for sure the case if either of your parents were addicts. Something in your particular makeup passed more than the possibility of a damaging dependency on to you. It passed the actual spirit and nature of the addiction itself. So do not try to remain addiction free with your willpower alone. Seek out organic solutions as well as psychological and spiritual ones to reach your goal of living an addiction free life.

A Few Thoughts I Have on this Insight:

Share your thoughts on this discussion.

_____

_____

_____

_____

_____

_____

_____

_____

_____

_____

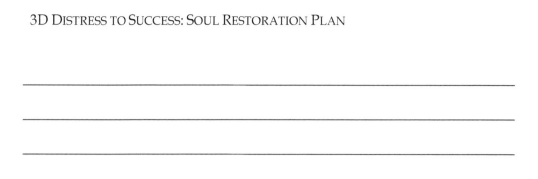 IS FOR YOU

One final note on the 3D Process for those who wonder if it is for them. Addiction takes many forms. In later guides, definitions show how. Addiction venerates what is loved and cherished. The object so adored consumes all of the affections and preoccupations. Dependency decrees the desires, commands the will, and orchestrates the actions. Addiction creates an tolerable enslavement that is perceived as being more rewarding and reliable than real life. Its gratification is akin to that received from a spiritual experience, or a deity. Addicts face all life's events with their addictions. They resolve all their difficulties through it, and mark their breakthroughs with it.

- When hurt, they turn to it.
- When happy, they celebrate with it.
- When confused, they substitute answers for it.
- When overwhelmed, they find solace in it.

No matter what the occasion, practicing the addiction or compulsion takes precedence over all else. Addiction redefines how normal human experiences are lived. What defines the addiction eventually defines the addict and three terms identify it.

Compulsive dependencies rely on four E's: exasperation, extremes, exaggeration, and excess. Everything is to the extreme with an addict. Excess is the only way their extreme appetites are satisfied. Exasperation with life's events justify exaggerated consolation, comfort, escape, or reward.

Addiction also takes away the stigma of insignificance by convincing its victims that who they are and what they do does not matter. The enslaving spirit assures them that neither of these should be a concern. The reverse of this emphasizes the appearance rather than the feelings. It deludes other victims into seeing themselves only one way. The way that observing an admired object or person made them feel. In this instance, the addiction takes the form of obsessiveness. A crippling or appalling low self esteem tricks self loathers into self destruction and practices that debilitate the body.

Think On This:

All addictions deprive their sufferers of contentment so deliverance is the last thing they imagine, until the best part of them is disfigured or devastated.

6 Ways This Discussion Recalls My Addiction Path for Me:

1.

2.

3.

4.

5.

6.

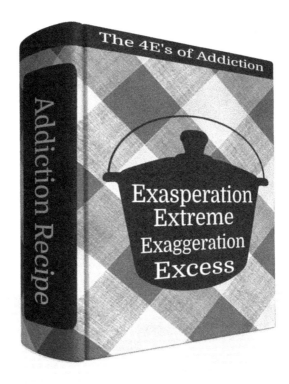

ADDICTION SHARES NOTHING AND TAKES EVERYTHING

Life stops for the addiction. Truth dies on the altar of the addiction. Identity is lost, integrity destroyed, and credibility shattered by the addiction. Vows are made and broken because of it. Prayers are made to and for it, and souls are consumed by it. Much of the addict's culture aligns completely with the spiritual practices of worship and ritual. From its compulsory drives to the soul's sacrifice, these are what classify it as idolatry. Addictive substances can be drugs, alcohol, food, bodily mutilation, or deforming cosmetics. Addictive behaviors can be sex, anger, rage, gossip, abuse, even slaughter. Addictive activities can extend to any extreme practice or habit that takes the place of everything else, especially a wholesome, balanced and productive lifestyle. People

43

can be addicted to fear and even optimism because the two exercised in the extreme can motivate reckless behavior. Fear is caution in excess; optimism's excess is unchecked belief in something that fails more than it succeeds.

Christians can be addicted to groundless faith that continually disappoints them because it has no prospects for material return. The gambler's faith for instance is reckless optimism. It is an unrealistice expectation of an undeserved reward.

The fearful are halted by debilitating hesitancy that shuts them out of opportunities or prevents them from overcoming life's obstacles. Whatever constricts the human experience to a single preoccupation or obsession qualifies as an addiction. If that preoccupation subsists on other's pain

"Truth dies on the altar of addiction."

and cost, it further fits the definition of an addiction because of what it produces in its victims and those that care for them, which is suffering and loss. This is especially true if the obsession precludes responsible actions and promotes isolation. All of it stems from the heart's commands to the will to see to its sorrows. The heart charges the volitional side of the human soul to provide for its desires, to recompense its offenses, or to mitigate its deprivation.

Heart ⊃Soul ⊃ Mind ⊃ Impact: ₃

Share your thoughts on this discussion.

_____

_____

_____

_____

_____

_____

₃ INTEGRITY AND FIDELITY

To maintain its integrity and not compromise its fidelity to the Lord that inspired it, the 3D Process goes beneath the surface, and often beneath the intelligence at first. It is based on scripture's assertion that the ax must be laid to the root of a problem, and that the source of all issues lies in the human heart. Subsequently, all 3D actions and encounters with its sufferers target the two root causes of soul bondage, the Savior's term for addiction. The first root is *idolatry*; the second root is *soul vow revenge*. The 3D approach treats the addiction as a tantrum and a revenge rampage because it receives its permission from the human will. The first root comes from abandoning Jesus Christ to worship and adore something else. Sometimes it is a direct path to addiction, and, at other times, the idolatry outcome takes a less direct route. The second root is assigning your willpower to enforce your decision to

45

evade life through addiction. Often, naïve souls fall into addiction through a fascination with what they believe is a more glamorous way to live.

EMULATION AND ASPIRATION CAN FOSTER ADDICTIONS

A lifestyle that presents itself as more appealing than the Lord's, when led, ends up addicting its admirers. Many young people fall prey to addiction this way. Some of them so admire a certain lifestyle that they conform their own life to it to emulate it. If some sort of dependency is part of it, like alcohol, drugs, perversion, or pleasure seeking, the admirer adopts it as well to imitate the object of their fascination. Another way addiction enters is through the union of the gullible with an addictive character or a relationship. This is when an ordinarily overlooked person comes to the attention of a venerated figure in their world. This can be a mentor, a love interest, or a role model. How the adored figure lives first tantalizes the admirer who slavishly emulates their ways. If dependency is a factor in that admiration, the impressionable soul will fall victim to its captivity. Any one or combination of these possibilities can be ascribed to the power to draw a soul into bondage to a doomed god.

THE SOUL VOW ROOT

The second root cause, the *soul vow*, really enforces the first captor, *idolatry*. In the case of the soul vow, anger, disappointment, hurt, abuse, and betrayal, along with a host of other soul traumas, create an early platform for possible addiction in the future. Anger with parents, the Lord, friends, family, or with life itself easily convinces a sorrowful soul that none of these powerful authorities can be confronted directly. The silent sufferer, in order to vent ire or frustration, turns inward to punish perceived culprits by association. They are drawn into a type of vicarious enslavement. The people who love them are obliged to watch the addicts in their lives self destruct. A quiet resolve makes sure the cause of their pain feels it vicariously. If the addict is a child, a spouse, a sibling, or a dear friend, watching a beloved soul self destruct is hard. Should the addict plunder the household goods and economy as well, the hardship is compounded by loss, debt, thefts, and so forth.

So in addition to standing by helplessly watching it, loved ones get to pay for their part in an addict's real or imagined pain in other ways. In this respect, the affected people bear the brunt of the person's self destruction by having their own lives turned upside down because of it. Voiced aloud or not, the sorrowful soul cannot help but reproduce that sorrow in other's lives because hurting people hurt people. Those closest to them become the targets and pillars of the addiction that is born from some emotional conflict the soul has with members of the family, close friends or mentors, distant relatives, or simply the institution that will not let them off the hook for a distasteful obligation.

THE COMPULSORY PLIGHT OF THE SORROWFUL SOUL

The mysterious villain in most addictions is "hope deferred". A lengthy discussion unmasking this culprit comes later in your deliverance process. However, at the outset, you should know that addictions mask sorrowful emotions that treat soul damage with

47

compulsory acts or behaviors. When the cause of the pain is not delayed hope or constant disappointments, but rather the result of a trauma or abuse that seeks to be relieved, deferred hope may be strictly tied to the need to relieve the soul's ache to cease reliving the ordeal that caused it. Notice the use of the word *relieved* instead of *healed*. This alteration is deliberate to differentiate the <u>temporariness</u> of the addiction from the <u>permanence</u> of deliverance. Remember this distinction as you go through the 3D Process. You should know emphatically that the two are entirely different with the word permanence being the determining factor.

When soul damage is caused by an assault, abuse, or trauma, the answer to its anguish is some kind of an obsession. A fixation or fascination is born out of a despair initiated by some or many disappointments. It is true that everyone has some sort of obsession that helps them temper soul pain and manage life's upsets. It is when the obsession consumes the thoughts and drives the impulses to oppose your well being and fruitfulness in life that they take on an unhealthy effect. In this case, they inhibit your freewill's ability to function as required and instead compel you to focus on things detrimental to your personal security or stability. These, as far as God is concerned, go right to the heart's archives: that place where sorrowful memories related to unsettling issues and incidents are catalogued and submerged.

Cunningly, the soul revises the events that scarred it to disguise them to enable you to keep going in life. Soul hurt revisions may take the form of dependencies, misconduct, excessive fears or imaginations, passive or aggressive vengefulness. If the cause of the disturbance was severe enough or so prolonged that coping habits were formed to survive it, some things as commonplace as sabotage, constant drama, or calamity can be the emotional revision executed.

Believe it or not, those with wounded emotions cannot recreate or dramatize their pain enough. Suffering souls can become addicted to chronic life upheavals. That perverse delight drives them to continually make life unpleasant for others. In these instances, the sorrowed soul keeps trouble brewing or cannot seem to stay out of it. They are fussy, intolerant, vindictive and difficult to relate to in life. Belligerence, impudence, or sarcasm characterizes many of their behaviors which compel them to constantly "get before they get got," so to speak. Other revisions are fearfulness, skepticism, cynicism, and aloofness, all put into operation to stay out of harm's way. These revisions allow the wounded to maintain a healthy distance between life's inescapable and their soul's vulnerabilities; this is conduct which is adopted to keep life at arm's length. Emotionally distressed people keep things in an uproar to calm the turbulence raging on the inside. This emotional modification tactic is a peculiar soul logic. It seeks to create a louder mayhem outside in order to drown out the endless chaos going on within the soul.

Heart ⊃Soul ⊃ Mind ⊃ Impact: D

Share your thoughts on this discussion.

_____

_____

_____

_____

EMOTIONALLY REVISED PAIN MEMORIES

All of the memory revisions mentioned above reiterate soul pain and announce it to the world, even if they do so cryptically. Insightful observers or skilled professionals perceptively interpret your soul's sorrow from your behaviors. The experienced ones can tap into your inner, unvoicable suffering. Emotional memory revisions serve as soul soothers you contrived to prop you up and push you forward in life, even if dysfunctionally. Sometimes soul soothers are concealed under a veneer of joy, compulsive drive, inexplicable irritability, or similar conduct to camouflage your sentiments from the world. These are your passive soul soothers. Others take a decided public approach. This sorrowful soul wants the world to know its pain and its path of relief. Public soothers are crafted to be blatant and are exhibitionist in nature. They take the form of bad or destructive habits, angry outbursts, impatience or indecency, a short temper, or chronic frustrations[1].

Some soul soothers or obsessive maneuvers only manifest during the day, others exclusively at the end of the day or at night. Of this sort, is excessive partying, intoxication, sexual compulsions or other demoralizing conduct. They goad your impulses to ensure your life decomposes and eventually demolishes. The first point of

---

[1] This occurs when you keep sabotaging yourself without realizing it.

attack is your body, the goads push you into unsafe or excessive behaviors or acts that break the seal on your well being. Quickly morphing into full blown addictions, your obsessions can feed your sorrow or relieve its effects. Whichever it is, and at times it can be both, every one of them contributes to the drama that makes up the plight of the sorrowful soul. No matter how public the life or superficially popular a person is, the sorrowful soul feels inwardly alienated and emotionally isolated from the world. Until the causative agony is resolved in a healthy way, this soul will find itself gripped in a downward spiral, unable to halt the obsession it only composed to evade an unbearable heartache.

YOUR CHOSEN SOUL SOOTHERS

The soul soothers you choose spur the impulsive behaviors that satisfy the obsession that emerged from what painfully disappointed you. The choices come from imaginations, desperation, deprivation, or denial. If something fascinated you just prior to or right after a painful ordeal, it can become a comforting soul soother. If the ordeal sprung from desperation or deprivation, the immediate soul soother will satisfy these and make up rules to continue doing so in the future either through provision or prevention. If a heartache collided with or was caused by something you wanted, then, in the future, whatever counteracts what was denied you becomes your soul soother of choice.

The practices or habits you engage to soothe your soul immediately after a traumatic ordeal make perfect sense to you. At least it did at the time you settled on its consolation. These gave you the temporary relief you sought to ease the sorrow in your soul. Emotional edicts may manifest differently from the heart's resolve because the edict must commission the soul which in turn commands the body. Soul commands program the mind according to the will by issuing orders to the body that provoke the appetites. These show up as the 4E's revealed in the Addiction Recipe book. In addition to excess, extremes, exasperation and exaggeration, they appear as fantastical escapes or uncontrollable self-gratification (gossiping, lying, drugs, anger, manipulations, eating, abuse, stealing, or sex, to name a few). However distasteful or destructive they may be on the surface, the root of the matter is a sorrowful soul seeking to alleviate or cope with throbbing resentments spurred by disappointment.

Heart ⊃Soul ⊃ Mind ⊃ Impact: D3

Share your thoughts on this discussion.

_____

_____

_____

_____

_____

_____

_____

_____

_____

_____

THE POWER OF EMOTIONAL DISAPPOINTMENT

Disappointments crush expectancy, and, if repeated or extensive enough, they stifle hope. Soul sorrow is a response to deeply submerged reactions to disappointments. An ongoing dynamic inwardly resolves the anger, wrath, embarrassment, offense or other negative emotion caused by a painful, threatening, or infuriating incident. Deserved or not, the heart reacts to anything that is discordant with its whims or vows, its peace or pursuits. A masterful repository, the human heart registers and reacts to *everything* that penetrates it, which is why the Lord tells us to guard it with all diligence. The human heart is the conductor of the soul that is designed to prevent or relieve emotional discomforts and seek remedies for whatever affects it.

The heart's defenses respond to these somewhat like the white blood cells of the body that immediately go to work soothing physical wounds. It is at this point the addiction option gets its start because resolving emotional hurt and sorrow takes priority over all else in the emotional self. The cogs and wheels depict your emotional apothecary's results how they respond to it to inseminate your addiction and afterward justify its maintenance.

Resolution decrees the solution; relief provides the support or aid that releases the heart to repair itself and end its sorrows. The remedy is the actual substance or treatment that restores calm or achieves satisfaction in response to what upset the heart. Addictions, indeed dependencies of all kinds, compound a unique sentient apothecary that blends the most impactful (positive or negative) emissions of the heart with the most rewarding expressions or pursuits.

1. **RESOLUTION: Decrees the solution.**
2. **RELIEF: Provides the support/aid that repairs**
3. **REMEDY: Substance or treatment that restores calm**

The heart's emotional intelligence is fueled by this apothecary mix. Once composed, the apothecary floods the soul. In the same way that the human heart floods the rest of the physical body with its life sustaining flow—blood, its immaterial but nonetheless earthly counterpart does the same with the emotions. Thus, it pumps the issues of life to the soul which in turn dumps its content into the flesh, beginning with the brain. This realization is a good place to do a bit of introspection. Start by researching your memories to isolate what decree, support or aid, substance or treatment could have possibly commanded your addiction.

Heart ⊃Soul ⊃ Mind ⊃ Impact: D₃

Share your thoughts on this discussion.

_____

_____

_____

_____

_____

_____

_____

TREATING THE SORROWFUL HEART

The sorrowed heart, once the heat of a painful moment passes, promptly goes to work on its wounds. Its processes include a search for ways to safeguard its access points to stop repeats of what wounded it. This is the resolve stage. If the will is barred from carrying out this assignment due to oppression or some other threat or detriment, it settles the sorrow with a determination that forges heart vows. In this instance, the resolve substitutes immediate or enduring solutions with obsessions that suppress the memory and reduce the pain until a more effective action can be taken. This course of treatment rests on the reality that nothing God has created ever really dissolves. If nothing overt can be done at the moment or shortly after, the will is charged by the heart to wait, its second best option. The will delays the heart's resolution if the answer desired is impossible at the time of the offense, but it stays alert for the opportunity to perform the heart's emotional tasks.

Although the desire to react to a distressing incident arises in the moment or shortly thereafter, unfavorable circumstances can demand it be postponed for a more opportune time. That is why people can suddenly switch their behavior in certain matters and act totally inconsistent with their normal personality. A shrewd emotional instrument, the emotional heart seizes opportunity to right a wrong done to it. At the most auspicious time, it moves the will to implement a resolution it decided on long ago. If the soul can carry out its resolution scheme with the one that caused the pain, well and good. If not, anything that revives the painful torment and the heart vow presolved to treat it becomes its target.

Irrational or not, the circumstances that appear most recuperative to the emotional self are enough to set the heart's long standing, long awaited resolves in motion. That is what sorrowful hearts do; they postpone what present circumstances prohibit them from fixing in the moment. But they are always on the lookout for the most opportune time (or incident) to put into effect postponed emotional dictates buried in the heart. To ride out the waiting period, the heart concocts emotional bandaids to soothe the soul's cry for relief. Once the most suitable bandaid is chosen and applied, it turns to pacifying its anguish and burying the torment. The heart's many chambers file away everything it just did and what happened to it for a better healing day, which could take a bit. This all brings us to the last step in the process. *Forgetting*.

Heart ⮌Soul ⮌ Mind ⮌ Impact: D₃

Share your thoughts on this discussion.

_____

_____

_____

_____

_____

_____

_____

THE COMMAND TO FORGET

The last step in this process is forgetting, what the previous emotional sequences were appointed to do. The debilitating ordeal that bruised and scarred the soul must be buried to halt the torment of reliving it. That calls for suppressing the memory to permit a return to the business of living. Although, until healing and deliverance are complete, it is more like going through the motions. In this scenario, the most important thing is keeping intimidating threats and emotional discomforts away. Once the best solution is found, the next step is to build walls around it. This stage involves identifying and selecting the most resistant guards to protect the soul's entryways and the heart's tender spots. The guards chosen are typically a contrived mix of preferred beliefs, distracting activities, perverted passions, and obsessive pursuits. Any one or all of these are adopted to stave off future emotional distresses. They also conceal deep within the memory chambers, guarding the sorrowful event causing the soul's trouble.

Once enacted, these assure the soul the maximum contentment possible from the solutions chosen. Willpower, imagination, and intelligence all participate in this process. The edict is to forget what disrupted life and hindered the ability to live it to the full. Every emotional tactic chosen is for the sorrowed soul to get back to the basics of life. To protect its elaborate defense system and see that nothing, roots out the vulnerability that threw it into deep disappointment, a therapeutic emotional complex is formed. Damaged souls lay an unnoticeable network of intolerances, or excesses that shield the heart's tender spots from the real world. That foundation scripts the soul's future addictive permissions. A predictive script is created and reserved for later when all the elements that prime the soul for addiction or compulsions unite and mature enough to invoke them. Secretly, in many people, that script breeds the soul to addict when, or if, the right set of circumstances present themselves.

Heart ⊃Soul ⊃ Mind ⊃ Impact: ℝ₃

Share your thoughts on this discussion.

_____

_____

_____

_____

_____

_____

_____

_____

THE DISGUISE

Earlier, two inner turmoils of the sorrowful soul were identified as alienation and isolation. On the surface, the sorrowful soul appears happy, alert, and well composed. This demeanor is genuine until the real or imagined threat to its security surfaces. Then all sorts of flags, bells, and whistles go off to set in motion the elaborate machine concocted to protect the emotions and shield the heart from its deepest fear, which is disappointment. How does it show up? The dreaded disappointment panic shows up disguised as risky (or risqué) behavior patterns, rigid decisions, irrational choices, and uncontrollable (and often illogical) push-back when emotional dangers surface. Under these circumstances, the submerged emotional operating system monitoring the feelings is aroused. Any one or combination of the signatures just mentioned sounds the alarm and sends the soul's defenses into full alert. Touchiness, disagreeableness, dissension, and arguments are the first responses. These are followed by distrust, accusation, criticism, and obstinacy; the last one, obstinacy, is the shutdown as the person's emotional doors and gates slam shut. The preprogrammed intolerances and excess guards are doing their job

59

well because outward misconduct aimed at protecting them shoos a lot of people away.

Meanwhile, mentally other things are happening. The thoughts are calling for immediate release or relief. What has been assigned to the will is authorized to search the heart's predetermined solutions for its healing or defense responses. This process may take days or weeks, sometimes even years. The reserved answers are hardly ever immediate because the moment the attack is happening, the only thing the soul is doing is fending it off. Returning to a less agitated frame of mind is the first order of business. It is not until later that recalling and reliving the incident occurs. Then the soul's solutions to its sorrows looks to the wounded heart to treat its wounds, the way the mind will when the physical body's assaults are over. When survival can give way to recovery, the processes explained above receives the command to repair, restore, and reseal the broken heart and all that it controls.

Heart ⊃Soul ⊃ Mind ⊃ Impact: B3

Share your thoughts on this discussion.

_____

_____

_____

_____

_____

End of Book 1, Stage 1

This is the end of the 3D Distress to Success Soul Restoration Plan. The guide you just completed, Book 1, Stage 1, introduced you to the journey you will undertake to free your soul from addictions and compulsions. Before completing this stage, go over the Stage 1 review—Reset Your Mind. Use it to memorize the principles you must apply to begin your distress to success process. The activity can be called "process blending" because it lets you enfold in your soul what you have learned on your journey so far. Your goal is to discover the strongholds you must treat to get your soul to lose its appetite for your addictive or compulsive behaviors. The purpose of the material you just finished is to retrain your heart to begin to, better yet, desire to think, feel, and crave to be addiction free. Once you complete your exercise, spend time with your coach and training mates reviewing what you have learned and preparing yourself for Book 2, Stage 2.

Decision

STAGE 1-- RESET YOUR MIND

1.	The Christ Distinctive	*Stay within Christ*
2.	The Path to Dependency	*You made the decision to addict*
3.	The Addict's Intelligence	*Addiction takes (or makes) a remarkable salesperson*
4.	How God Delivers a Soul	*He re-applies eternity's codes of life*
5.	To Be Free	*The addicted saint must repent*
6.	Ð Integrity and Fidelity	*Goes beneath the surface, and often beneath the intelligence at first*
7.	The First Root Cause of Addiction	*Soul Trauma*
8.	The Second Cause of Addiction	*Idolatry*
9.	The Third Root Cause of Addiction	*The Soul Vow*
10.	3D Is for You	*Because addiction takes many forms*

YOUR 3D PROCESS JOURNAL

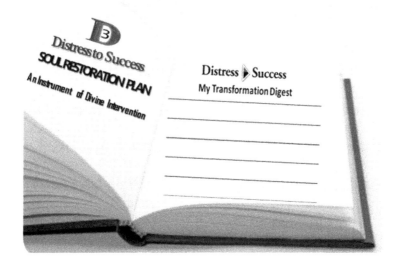

Transformation Digest 1

Distress ▶ Success

Transformation Digest 2

Distress ▶ Success

Transformation Digest 3

Distress  Success

Transformation Digest 4

Distress  Success

Transformation Digest 5

Distress ▶ Success

Transformation Digest 6

Transformation Digest 7

Distress ▶ Success

Transformation Digest 8

Distress  Success

Transformation Digest 9

Distress  Success

Transformation Digest 10

Distress ▶ Success

Soul Restoration Plan

Transformation Task: A/V Session, Supplement

Audio-Video Listening Review Guide

Session Name		Your Name	
	Session Number		
Focus			
Listening Goal			

Assigned Pre-Course Reading from Scriptures and/or Text

No.	Scripture Passage(s)/Text	Purpose	Relevance	Knowledge/Skill Value
1.				
2.				
3.				
4.				
5.				

Teaching's Title

Lecture Topic

Lecturer Name

Lecturer Office

**Lecture
Emphasis**

Did the speaker announce the teaching's title?   Yes   No. What was the title given?

Did Teaching Match Title?   Yes   No

Summarize What is Required of You in This Assignment

Were there any significant scriptures used in the tape lecture?   Yes   No. If so, list them below.

1.	2.	3.
4.	5.	6.

In one sentence or less, give what you recognized to be the apparent connections between the stated scriptures you identified and the overall message's benefit to your transformation.

A.

B.

C.

The final requirement is to identify any specific enrichment you received as well as how you know you received them. Lastly, you will be asked for a commentary statement on the lecture in relation to its contribution to your overall progress in the study entitled.

Your Name

Today's Date

Date Assignment is Due _____

Submit to Your Success Coach

3D PROCESS MATERIALS

If you are working with a coach, please consult them before purchasing resources.

Recommended Audio Resources

Time to be Healed

The Soul of Success: The Come-Back Plan

The Soul of Success: Emotions

The Soul of Success: Destiny

Finding Your Worth in God

Time to Control Your Mind

Facing Giants

Embrace the Power of Grace

The Power of Virtue

The Mysteries of Success I and II

Love is Supernatural

Living Up to the God in You

Books and Short-Reads

The 3D Series

The Soul of Success Devotional

When God Goes Silent

Accessing Your Resources

Visit www.drpaulaprice.com. Choose "SHOP" to access the online store.

Start Your 3D Soul Restoration Program
Stage-by-Stage Mentorship and Training

The *3D Soul Restoration Program* takes you through a step-by-step healing and restorative journey to wholeness and success. Each stage is combined with hands-on mentorship and coaching, listening and learning, activities, special projects and more. There is a deep desire in each one of us to do what God has called us to do and walk in the fullness of what He has planned for our lives. However, the journey is not always easy, and the answers are not always clear. We all reach a point in our walk with the Lord where we need clarity, focus, or direction. The 3D program uses a unique *teach-talk-touch* approach to help you identify where you are to unearth what it is that keeps you from moving forward in God.

Choosing a Restoration Mentor

Our stage-by-stage 3D restoration programs connect you with a certified mentor or coach who will walk you through your restoration plan step by step, if you desire. Although you can work through each guide on your own, you can choose to obtain your deliverance and healing through taking advantage of our entire program; all you have to do is sign up for monthly mentorship sessions. During your journey, you will be required to have regular check-ins. At the start, you will receive a customized deliverance plan to suit your unique needs. Your mentor is specifically trained in the 3D process and has successfully met all the qualifications.

Registering for a 3D Program

To learn more about starting a program, contact a PPM Global Resources representative at www.ppmglobalresources.com to schedule a consultation, call 877-419-1299, or email us at admin@ppmglobalresources.com.

ABOUT THE AUTHOR

Paula A. Price is a strong and widely acknowledged international voice on the subject of apostolic and prophetic ministry. She is recognized as a modern-day apostle with a potent prophetic anointing. Active in full-time ministry since 1985, she has founded and established three churches, an apostolic and prophetic Bible institute, a publication company, consulting firm, and global collaborative network linking apostles and prophets for kingdom vision and ventures. Through this international ministry, she has transformed the lives of many through her wisdom and revelation of God's kingdom.

As a former sales and marketing executive, Dr. Price effectively blends ministerial and entrepreneurial applications in her ministry to enrich and empower a diverse audience with the skills and abilities to take kingdoms for the Lord Jesus Christ. Her strength? Empowering lives with God's Wisdom. As a lecturer, teacher, curriculum developer and business trainer, Dr. Price globally consults Christian businesses, churches, schools and assemblies. Over a 30-year period, Dr. Price has developed a superior curriculum to train Christian ministers and professionals, particularly the apostle and the prophet. Her programs are often used in both secular and non-secular environments worldwide. Although she has written over 25 books, manuals, and other course material on the apostolic and prophetic, she is most recognized for her unique 1,600-term *Prophet's Dictionary* and her concise prophetic training manual entitled *The Prophet's Handbook*. Other publications include *The ABC's of Apostleship*, a practical guide to the fundamentals of modern apostleship; *Divine Order for Spiritual Dominance*, a five-fold ministry tool; *Eternity's Generals*, an explanation of today's apostle; and *When God Goes Silent: Living Life Without God's Voice*. Her latest works include *Before the Garden, God's Eternal Continuum* and the *3D Soul Restoration Plan* that helps addicts and compulsives take their life from distress to success. The latter includes spiritual and business soul of success training.

In 2002, Dr. Price created one of the most valuable tools for Christian Ministry called the Standardized Ministry Assessment series. It is a patent pending, destiny discovery tool that tells people who they are in God, what He created them to do, and how He created them to do it. The assessment series pinpoints those called to the church, its pulpit or other ministries, and those who would better serve the Lord outside of the church.

Beside this, Dr. Price has also developed credentialing tools for ministers and professionals, commissioning criteria and practices, along with ceremony proceedings for apostles and prophets. To complement these, she designed extensive educational programs for the entire five-fold officers and their teams.

In addition to her vast experience, Dr. Price has a D.Min. and a Ph.D. in Religious Education from Word of Truth Seminary in Alabama. She is also a wife, mother of three daughters, and the grandmother of two.

Printed in the USA
CPSIA information can be obtained
at www.ICGtesting.com
LVHW081039220124
769607LV00038B/877